Nine Ways To Empower Yourself Today

Published and distributed in the United States by Alrick Douglas, Paterson, New Jersey

Copyright © 2019 by Alrick Douglas, MA

All rights reserved. No parts of this book be reproduced by any mechanical, photographic, or electronic process, or in the form of phonographic recording; nor may it be stored in a retrieval system, transmitted, or otherwise be copied for public or private use – other than for "fair use" as brief quotations embodied in articles and reviews – without prior written permission of the publisher.

The author intends to offer information of a general nature to help you in your quest to advocate for your self-esteem and well-being. In the event you use any of the information in this book for yourself, which is your constitutional right, the author or publisher assume no responsibility for your actions.

Cover Design – The Self-Publishing Maven
Editing and Layout – The Self-Publishing Maven
Interior Design – Istvan Szabo, Ifj. (Sapphire Guardian Intl.)
ISBN – 978-1-7334310-2-6

Printed in the United States of America

Nine Ways To Empower Yourself Today

Alrick Douglas, MA

Acknowledgments

I am forever grateful for those individuals who supported me on this amazing journey. I appreciate the openness and trust demonstrated that allowed me to empower those who are ready to make meaningful change in their lives.

I thank my wife Candice, for being such a source of strength and private inspiration as I take my message public. She always encourages me to be the best version of myself and not be easily shaken. Her private empowerment allows me to be available to many.

I thank Pastor Lina and Bishop Dale Guarjena for their remarkable impact on my life and for giving me a platform to empower others. I am forever grateful for the generosity of Rajae Powis, Gustav Kofi Sam and Malik Smith in getting this project off the ground. They have all had personal success through their willingness to change after being empowered.

Dedication

I dedicate this book to all my clients who have experienced personal growth and change in their social and emotional development. I also want to dedicate this book to individuals who at times feel a sense of aloneness with their challenges. I want to use these tips to encourage them that their best days are before them and not behind them.

Contents

Introduction 7

Way One: Staying Focused versus Feelings 9

Way Two: Appreciate Timing 12

Way Three: Be Creative 16

Way Four: Take The Leap 19

Way Five: Collaborate 21

Way Six: Understand NO Means- Next Option 23

Way Seven: Become Fearless 26

Way Eight: Embrace Your Humanity 28

Way Nine: Maintain Boundaries 31

Conclusion 33

Notes 35

Introduction

We all come to a time in our life where we need to be and feel empowered. There are several definitions to the word, but the one fits with the context of this book is, "make (someone) stronger and more confident, especially in controlling their life and claiming their rights."

Being in control of your physical, mental, and emotional state and living your life to the fullest are both tied to empowerment and freedom. As we receive information to make us stronger and more confident, the personal reward is to take that information and move toward our personal goals and desires, as well as create growth and change.

Nine Ways To Empower Yourself Today is a toolbox to put in your positive arsenal so you can stay on the track of consistent empowerment. Filled with real-life examples of people I know and admire from afar, the contents the share of what I've learned from personally doing, watching as well as working with friends, families, and personal clients who desired to be at a particular stage in their lives. To meet any goal, empowerment is necessary.

Additionally, this book will challenge you to say 'No' to what doesn't serve you, set boundaries, follow your dreams, take leaps (even when scared) and persevere toward success.

The word 'empower' is a verb, but some of the synonym words are, emancipate, unyoke, unfetter, unshackle, unchain, and set free. I believe that no one sets out to be shackled, chained, or yoked, so it's important to seek 'empowerment' as often as possible.

I can safely say that you are looking for more empowerment because you have this book in your possession. There is much information and many tools out there to keep you on track, but I am excited you decided to read my perspective on the subject. The goal is to get stronger, more confident, and be free to be the best version of you. Here is one more seed to help you get there.

Let's go!

Way One:
Staying Focused versus Feelings

Blockbuster versus Netflix

This story is an example of the importance of staying focused on the prize versus walking in what you feel. Let's look at the back story to this moment.

Blockbuster was the place where people went for all their movie choices to rent and buy. The stores were located nationally, internationally, and thrived on people coming to the store and having a great experience. They were approached by a young man who had an idea for Blockbuster to expand their business to start shipping movies to homes of those who couldn't get to the store. The idea would give them another leg to their business and cater to the changing times where people were beginning to order online more. Blockbuster 'felt' they should keep their same model and open stores instead of getting 'focused' on expanding their brand and business. They decided to reject the young man who came to them with the idea.

Empowering Moment!

You may have a thought, idea, invention, etc., that you believe is awesome but may face rejection in the moment of sharing. Don't get discouraged. Stay focused! The focus your vision demands will require defending even in the face of rejection. Again, Blockbuster rejected a deal that would transform their business and expand their company. However, those who carried the vision of Netflix were not deterred. They 'refocused' and persisted with the idea. They went back to that place of conception and decided to take on the project themselves. The interesting part is, sometimes we turn to people we believe possess the resources and influence to propel our vision to the next level. Although they are successful and appear ready for what's next, they're not. Today Netflix has transformed from a rejected idea to multi-billion-dollar streaming company that now carries major influence in how we see movies. Blockbuster went out of business.

Empowerment Nuggets!

1. Know that dreamers often receive criticism.
2. You can't stop people from talking about you.
3. You can't stop people from rejecting you.
4. Protect your mental state.
5. Let your good work speak for you.
6. Identify distractions.
7. Reject stress.
8. Create strategies.
9. Stay focused on the prize.
10. Temper your feelings.

Sometimes rejection is not a sign that something is wrong with your idea; it simply means the person or place rejecting you cannot contain your greatness. Manage what you're feeling. Stay focused! You must reconcile within yourself that you are great so you can impact those in your environment.

Way Two:
Appreciate Timing

__Thomas Edison and Jeff Bezos__

The subtitle might sound a little weird with those words coupled together, but they fit the context of the overall message.

When you have a plan, appreciating timing will yield the return you desire and will last for more than a moment. Knowing the right timing secures that whatever lies ahead has already been prepared to handle. When we rush ahead of timing, the thing we have worked on or desired may not stand the test of time.

Thomas Edison

Thomas Edison is described as one of America's great inventors. We all know that he created the electric light bulb. It's safe to say that he is the father of appreciating timing. He is famous for the coined phrase, "I have not failed. I've just found 10,000 ways that won't work."

Jeff Bezos

Today, I don't think many people don't know about Amazon, the multi-billion-dollar company. The idea was a big dream that started in a small place and grew into an eCommerce giant. Jeff Bezos first launched Amazon in his garage. He had a vision of creating a selling company that would make shopping easy and whatever you want accessible nationally and internationally. He began with shipping books. Even though he started in a garage with one product type, his overall vision wasn't far off. He maintained patience with starting small and giving his vision time to grow. Today, Amazon trades with and ships products to countries all over the world with multiple fulfillment centers globally. Not only is Amazon an eCommerce giant, but it also is headed by the world's wealthiest man. Mr. Bezos now enjoys the story that he gave his idea and company time to grow.

Empowering Moment!

Failure to understand the importance of timing can frustrate your vision. As you work and plan, keep the fire and excitement ablaze. Never get ahead of yourself because it seems you are losing impact. In today's fast-paced world, like a microwave, everything needs to get hot in minutes. Do you have a microwave mentality? Ask yourself these questions:

1. Do I lack patience waiting for my dream to come to fruition?
2. Do I expect immediate returns in the time I invest?
3. Do I bounce back in times of set back or do I let frustration overwhelm my process?
4. Do I possess the creativity to adapt?
5. Do I appreciate the learning process within timing?

Our first 'way' discussed staying focused versus feelings. Thomas Edison and Jeff Bezos are our great examples of waiting, appreciating timing, and yielding results by staying consistent.

Empowerment Nuggets!

1. All seeds need time to grow.
2. Some visions are part of a marathon and not a sprint.

3. Celebrate your moments of progress within the process.
4. Pray for patience.
5. Stay in a posture of persistence.
6. Evaluate what doesn't work
7. Adapt to changes when necessary.
8. Striving for perfection can kill your passion.
9. Understand that creative blocks may occur.
10. Embrace moments of relaxation and recharging.

Now is a good time to look back at the book you thought about writing, the business you dreamed of starting or whatever great idea you've been holding due to timing. Perhaps, you were waiting for perfect conditions and resources. I have some good news! You have time to get back to work. Don't get stuck because it seems things are not working out at first; spend some time exploring.

Way Three:
Be Creative

<u>A Personal Story</u>

It took me some time to get to this space of sharing how to empower yourself and being creative.

My academic journey to obtaining a master's degree in counseling and leading today's youth and their families, and fostering personal growth and development showed me how much people need to be empowered and allowed to cultivate their creativity.

While mentoring teens, I garnered five years of experience as an in-home therapist and working with children diagnosed with autism and their families. I was able to empower my clients to steer their journeys to success, no matter what challenges they faced daily. Whether it was motivational speech, a social and emotional development group or mere individual or family session, I have used varied techniques to empower my clients to embrace the best version of their self.

The time came where I had to drink from a cup of creativity for myself when I decided to write my first book and move into the public speaking arena. I am excited to report this is the second book. However, my first one was a personal challenge. It's always easier to encourage others than yourself.

Empowerment Moment!

One of the obstacles on the journey to self-actualization is the tendency to measure who you're becoming in the lens of where others have been. In the planning stages, I tried to develop my company to model other motivational speakers. I realized that no matter how many videos I watched or success stories I read, they weren't in line to what I saw and imagined for myself. Although I went through a moment of wondering if I could write a book or create a company, I decided to take the leap, embrace, and unleash my creative ideas.

I learned creativity is like an open dam of free-flowing water released to take you places beyond what your abilities and mind can contain.

Empowerment Nuggets!

1. We are all one creative idea away from millionaire status.
2. Write the book.
3. Create the course.
4. Produce the event.
5. Your creativity will be tested.
6. Never throw away an idea, seek to tweak.
7. Take control over any anxiety.
8. Handle your creativity with care.
9. Know your worth.
10. Don't just seek mentorship, seek wisdom.

I had to learn that people were patiently waiting for me to show up. Instead of throwing away my idea of becoming an author, I tapped into my environment and connected with areas I saw my connections needed the most. I began to write to those areas with passion, and by the time I looked up, I had three chapters down. The moment I announced my first book, I had an overwhelming response. The community that is assigned to receive your creativity is waiting on you. Don't keep them waiting.

Way Four:
Take The Leap

Disney World

Who doesn't love Disney World? It is a magical place of beauty and where one can dream live and in color, at any time of the year. Walt Disney was already a giant in television, film, character creation and animation; however, he had an idea to create a live fantasy amusement park where children and parents could have fun and the dreams of tomorrow could be realized.

Focused, appreciating timing, expanding his creativity and 'leaping' to the next level, Disney theme park was born and had over three million visitors in its first year.

Empowerment Moment!

To attain the height of personal success, contrary voices must be silenced, fear must be squashed, and leaping is necessary.

Another way to look at leaping is by the example of a pregnant woman. She carries a child for nine months being uncomfortable at times and uncertain about motherhood and what the responsibility entails. However, she has decided to go forth in birthing greatness. Though painful, she appreciates the kicks and discomfort as evidence that her baby (her destiny to be a mother) is still alive and coming soon.

Empowerment Nuggets!

1. Silence the external noise of naysayers.
2. Silence the internal noise of self-defeating talk.
3. Doubt and Faith can't reside in the same place.
4. Get out of your comfort zone.
5. Uncertainty births creativity.
6. Think but don't overthink.
7. Don't harp on past failures.
8. Trust the process.
9. Enjoy the journey.
10. Keep leaping.

Leaping is sometimes the hardest thing to do as you navigate a change in life, but you will never know if the idea will work if you don't leap.

Way Five:
Collaborate

Is there someone whom you admire from afar and believe that collaboration would be a great thing for both of you? Has anyone approached you to collaborate on a project and you were apprehensive about making the connection?

Collaboration is the new currency and why do things by yourself if you don't have to.

I am a firm believer in the power of collaboration for it marries creativity to an existing or new perspective that can take you or your idea to the next level.

Empowerment Moment!

There are many, but here four good reasons why you should collaborate.

1. Access – can grant you access to people, places, and things that supports your idea or vision.
2. Innovative Ideas – opens the door to ideas you may not have otherwise thought of.

3. Productivity – we tend to be more results-driven when we accomplish goals with another person.
4. Helps Overcome Obstacles – when issues arise, you won't have to figure out the solution for yourself but will have the support needed to get over the hump.

Empowerment Exercise!

Of course, you want to be strategic in who you collaborate with and ensure that they possess the same vision and values needed for your idea. Pray about it and get to work right now — list five people, ministries, or organizations you would like to collaborate with on an idea.

1. _____
2. _____
3. _____
4. _____
5. _____

Way Six:
Understand NO Means - Next Option

From a toddler to an adult, the word 'NO' is associated with rejection. The truth is, we all want to have our desires satisfied without interruption. The word "No" tends to slow us down to a place of reflection of our choices. Hearing the word can also overwhelm, foster emotionalism, and block understanding. However, hearing "No" from people or places should activate new directions and inspiration. It takes a level of personal maturity to accept "denial" and see it as a greater opportunity to grow. The ability to rebound from disappointments, hinges on your willingness to see "No" as a booster to your creative imagination.

Empowerment Moment!

I once worked with a young adult who was trying to get recognized for his fashion design skills. The more he designed and submitted to various fashion houses, the more the responses came with critique, but not acceptance. He was disappointed, and I could relate to what he felt on a human level. However, I asked him, "What improvements did they recommend?" I saw what they were saying from a different perspective and pointed out to him, although the response was a "NO" the critiques carried "YES." The more he worked on improving and adapting the critiques in his designs, the better he became at his craft. Today he is working for a recognized fashion house.

Again, we must look at the denials we experience as an opportunity to grow and to be more creative. The word 'NO' means what is the 'Next Option' to get to your goal.

<u>Empowering Nuggets!</u>

1. 'NO' will make you ask more questions.
2. 'NO' will have you reevaluate your intentions.
3. 'NO' will have you reevaluate the reason behind what you desire.
4. 'NO' will force you out of your comfort zone.
5. 'NO' stimulates the imagination.
6. It is okay to accept the 'NO' for now.
7. NO' doesn't mean you're not capable.

8. 'NO' could mean you're not ready at this precise moment.
9. 'NO' is often dressed in opportunity.
10. Remember, 'NO' means 'Next Option.'

Way Seven:
Become Fearless

Have you ever pondered doing something you had never done before and was suddenly gripped by fear? You are not alone. Those who have accomplished great success took the risk of exploring what's on the other side of their fear. When we live life from a place of fear, we have settled for being on the sideline, cheering others on to victory, and wishing we dared to do what we see. Yes! Life is indeed better on the other side, but only those who take the leap encounter the better.

Empowering Moment!

I mentor a young adult diagnosed with Leukemia. He is single, wealthy, accomplished. He's just 25 years old and suddenly had to manage an illness that created a new normal in his life. I am impressed by his tenacity to push against the fear of death and still explore the possibilities that life has to offer. He encourages me personally by sharing his experiences and process of working to do what the doctor says. Leukemia is a lot to deal with; however, he decided to walk on the other side of his fear and love life by eating healthier and seeking great relationships with people. The diagnosis changed his perspective. He is now married and starting a family. He became fearless when he decided to reject the voice of fear, which robs inner victory.

In this case, the possibility of death is what pushed my mentee to live life. That may not be your situation, but let his example serve as a good reason for you to become fearless in life.

If you want to become fearless, those times when fear begins to creep in do the following:

Empowering Questions!

1. What am I afraid of?
2. What is the worst that can happen if I do this?
3. What do I need to do to reject the fear?
4. How can I be brave at this moment?

Overcoming fear is directly linked to 'leaping' like discussed in Way Four. Live life! Move forward!

Way Eight:
Embrace Your Humanity

Most people are very hard on themselves when they make mistakes. Whether it's friendships, marriages, employment, or business, we all make mistakes and must embrace that we are human. If your heart is sincere about the mistake or error, we shouldn't feel ashamed, isolated, and disconnected. Of course, we don't want to use humanity as an excuse to hurt or mislead people. However, embracing humanity indicates we are compassionate to ourselves and others.

How can you embrace your humanity today? For this 'way' we will combine 'empowering moment' and 'empowering nuggets' on how you can embrace your humanity daily?

1. Pray daily.
2. Be grateful.
3. Appreciate all, big and small.
4. Walk-in compassion for self and others.
5. Walk-in humility.

6. Identify your strengths and weaknesses and improve where necessary.
7. Permit yourself to be imperfect.
8. Unconditionally love yourself.
9. Embrace other cultures.
10. Share resources.
11. Be a mentor.
12. Seek and nurture meaningful relationships.
13. Don't be a victim.
14. Forgive self and others.
15. Seek to help others.

To elaborate on number 15 from the above, here is an example of how embracing humanity and helping others can impact their lives in a major way.

The movie Black Panther (2018) broke records at the box office. Fans were impressed by the movie but the lead, Chadwick Boseman, had an interesting story of how his life was touched by humanity. He shared there was a time when he was in college, and his funds were running low for tuition. He got a breakthrough when called to the Bursar office and was told his tuition was paid for by Denzel Washington. Floored by the generosity and never forgetting the blessing, he later had the opportunity to thank Denzel personally and is now one of today's best actors. Denzel Washington didn't know who Chadwick Boseman was; he simply wanted to help a young man out. Denzel helped to seal Chadwick's future.

God designed us to be good, not perfect. Embrace who you are.

Way Nine:
Maintain Boundaries

Maintaining healthy boundaries with people is essential to stay on the path of consistent empowerment. It's sad but true that not everyone that we contact should be connected to us. I have counseled people over my professional career who deal with immense regret because they have been emotionally scarred by people who they gave access way too early through relationships and business ventures. If you can attest to the same thing, you must do a better job in how you give people access to your life. When you set clear boundaries, those in your circle have a better understanding as to how far they can go and what they can access. Keep in mind that you can set boundaries for your personal space, emotions and thoughts, time and energy, and spirituality.

Empowerment Moment!

Manipulations often creep in when our boundaries are undefined. We must be vigilant and be on the lookout for manipulation, so those connected to us understand the rules that govern our existence. One of the challenges that come when dealing with manipulation is the choice of cutting vs. moving on. For your safety and emotional regulation, there comes a time when we must cut someone off for self-preservation. The truth is some relationships require an ending so we can hit the reset button and refocus on our dreams and vision.

In other instances, we may have to make a choice and move on with better awareness and appreciation for the lessons learned. How can you maintain boundaries with whom you come in contact?

Empowerment Nuggets!

1. Decide to do so.
2. Remember, you aren't empowered if you allow manipulation to take over.
3. Share your limits.
4. Be candid.
5. Be aware of your feelings.
6. Make yourself a priority.
7. Be assertive, not aggressive.
8. Seek help to maintain when needed.

Setting boundaries takes practice and courage, but I know you got this!

Conclusion

This book was designed to provide some quick tips on how you can become more empowered today. We discussed the importance of staying focused on your goals versus your feelings. I'm not saying you shouldn't feel, but it's important not to let your feelings overwhelm to the point of ruling your decisions.

We talked about appreciating the timing of things. The saying is true that Rome wasn't built in a day. Patience is paramount!

It's important to stay in a place of creativity. You never know where your creative side can take you and change your life. While in that creative space, it's important to take leaps toward your next.

It's great to take leaps, but even greater if you collaborate with others with certain personal and professional goals. Yes, you will meet a lot of people along the way, and some will say no, however, remember 'NO' means Next Option.

When moving to the next option, become fearless. Being scared is not of God.

Remember to embrace who you are and your humanity. The only one perfect is God.

Always maintain boundaries and protect your space.

Ultimately, I hope this tool opens a personal and self-discussion on personal growth, affirming self, positive self-talk, and walking in victory when we are all empowered, society benefits tremendously.

Notes

Nine Ways To Empower Yourself Today

Nine Ways To Empower Yourself Today